Rivers

Catherine Chambers

Heinemann Library
Chicago, Illinois

Designed by David Oakley
Illustrations by Tokay Interactive
Originated by Dot Gradations
Printed in Hong Kong/China

04 03 02 01 00
10 9 8 7 6 5 4 3 2 1

Library of Congress Cataloging-in-Publication Data

Chambers, Catherine, 1954-
     Rivers / Catherine Chambers.
          p. cm. – (Mapping earthforms)
     Includes bibliographical references (p.) and index.
     Summary: Examines the world's rivers, discussing how they were formed, what organisms live there, and how they are used by humans.
     ISBN 1-57572-527-4 (lib. bdg.)
     1. Rivers—Juvenile literature. [1. Rivers.] I. Title.

GB1203.8C53 2000
551.48'3—dc21   99-046853

Acknowledgments
The Publishers would like to thank the following for permission to reproduce photographs: Tony Stone Images, p. 4; Ecoscene/N. Hawkes, p. 5; Robert Harding Picture Library/E. Young, p. 6; Ecoscene/R. Greenwood, p. 9; Oxford Scientific Films/C. Lockwood/ Earth Scenes, p. 11; Minden Pictures, p. 13; Still Pictures/J. Schytte, p. 14; Oxford Scientific Films/G. Kidd, p. 16; Bruce Coleman Limited/A. Potts, p. 17; Oxford Scientific Films/H. and J. Beste, p. 18; Oxford Scientific Films/K. Ringland, p. 19; Robert Harding Picture Library/C. Bowman, p. 20; Still Pictures/P. Harrison, p. 23; Ecoscene/Gryniewicz, p. 24; Anthony King, p. 25; Robert Harding Picture Library, p. 26; Still Pictures/H. Schwarzbach, p. 29.

Cover photograph reproduced with permission of Robert Harding Picture Library.

Some words are shown in bold, **like this.** You can find out what they mean by looking in the glossary.

Contents

What Is a River?

A river is a body of flowing water. Sometimes it rushes and rages. At other times it flows slowly along. A river is always pulled by the earth's **gravity** from high ground down to a large lake or to the sea. A stream is a smaller body of water that flows into a river. We will see how a river and its streams make up a **river system**.

How did rivers begin?

Water began from gases that formed around the earth millions of years ago. Millions of years ago, too, mountain peaks rose when great **plates** of the earth's crust pushed together. The rain that fell on the mountains gathered in dips and cracks. It then began to flow as streams and rivers. We will find out how the earth's **water cycle** continues to make streams and rivers flow.

The Amazon is the second-longest river in the world. It is so long that it flows through many different **climates** and types of **vegetation.** It runs from the cold Andes mountains through hot **tropical** rain forests and into the Atlantic Ocean.

4

What do rivers look like?

Rivers begin on higher ground as streams, springs, or patches of soggy ground. As the water gathers, it flows down the mountainside, sometimes as a waterfall. As the slope flattens, the river still flows quickly. It also becomes wider. The river widens even more as it reaches a lake or the sea. Here it slows down. The force of the water and the pull of gravity help to carve shapes in the earth. We will see how rivers change the landscape and find out how rivers are always changing.

Life in and around rivers

Rivers teem with life. Plants thrive in and around them. Many kinds of animals live in or near the water. People could not have survived without rivers. We will see how living things have **adapted** to them. We will also discover how people have changed rivers and river landscapes around the world.

Plants, animals, and people must have water to live. Clean rivers like this one provide the perfect **habitat** for many living **species**. Polluted rivers have less oxygen in the water. This harms life in the river.

Rivers of the World

The world has millions of rivers and streams. Some rivers are tiny. Others flow a very long way through huge land masses called continents. For example, the continent of Africa has the mighty Nile River winding far down its eastern side. The Niger River cuts a curve through western Africa.

Rare rivers

Some areas of the world do not have rivers. The Sahara Desert in northern Africa is a good example. These areas do not have rivers because the **climate** is very dry. There is very little rain in these deserts. When rain does fall, it pours down. The rainstorms make rivers in the sand and dry rock. These rivers soon disappear when the sun shines on them and the dry winds blow. Then only dry river beds remain.

The Rocky Mountains stretch from Mexico to Canada. Part of the mountain range forms a **watershed** called the Continental Divide. It runs from Colorado north to Canada. The great Colorado River flows down the west side and runs through rocky desert and the Grand Canyon.

6

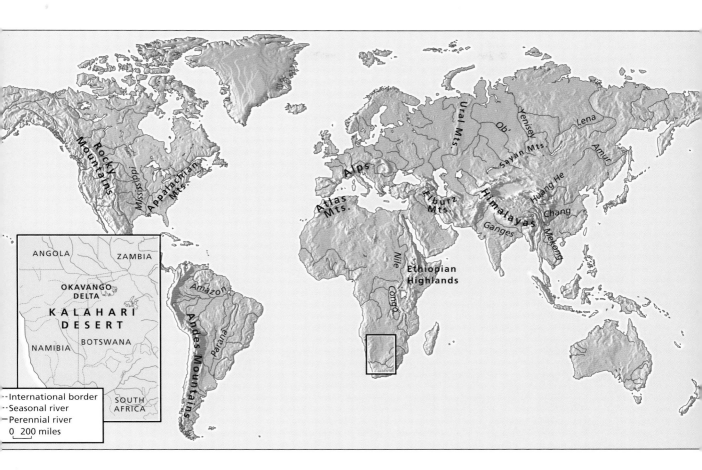

Some areas of the world, such as Botswana, have only two main seasons during the year. One season is dry; the other is wet. Rivers that flow only in the wet season are called seasonal rivers.

Mountains, rain, and rivers

Most long rivers flow from high mountains. The map on this page shows that many rivers flow down one side of the Andes in South America. This is because **trade winds** pick up moisture from the world's oceans and blow it toward the mountain range. The moisture turns into rain as it rises up the slope. The rain falls high on the mountain and flows back down in rivers. It is very dry on the other side of the mountain where the rain does not reach.

The main map shows the world's major rivers and mountain ranges. The inset map shows an area of southern Africa where there are many seasonal rivers.

7

The River System

A **river system** is made up of one major river and all the streams that flow into it. It is contained in a **drainage basin** with sloping sides. Each basin is separated from other river basins by the high rim or ridge of ground around it. This rim is called the **watershed.**

The river system is the water that can actually be seen in rivers and streams. But more water feeds the system from under the ground. The water soaks, or percolates, through the earth and soft rock. The percolated water and the river system above ground together are known as the river catchment area. But how does water continually feed the rivers and streams?

This is the river system of the Mississippi River. It covers much of the United States. Its **tributaries** include the Missouri River, which flows from the west, and the Ohio River, which flows from the east.

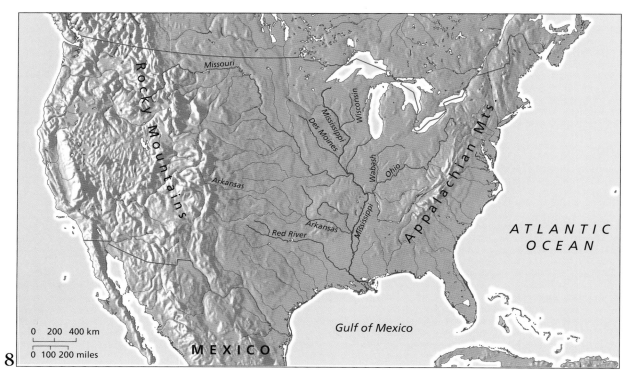

8

The earth's water cycle

There is always the same amount of water on Earth, but it comes in different forms. Much of it exists as liquid water in oceans, seas, lakes, rivers, or streams. Some of it exists as ice, frozen in polar ice caps or glaciers. Water can fall as rain, snow, or hail. At other times it is held in tiny droplets in clouds, mist, and fog. Sometimes water cannot be seen at all. When it is sunny, water from the oceans, seas, and lakes **evaporates** into the air. It rises as invisible **water vapor**. Plants also put water vapor into the air through holes in their leaves.

Water vapor often forms high clouds. As the clouds get even higher, the water in them cools and becomes water droplets. These fall as rain. The rain then fills streams and rivers, lakes and seas. Then, when the sun shines down on these waters, the same cycle happens again. The **water cycle** is also known as the hydrological cycle. It affects the whole world, including the dryest areas. Each river drainage basin has its own smaller water cycle, too.

The amount of water that can be seen on Earth changes all the time. In summer, the sun evaporates a lot of water. This leaves low rivers and lakes or even no rivers and lakes. In winter there is more rain and the rivers fill and flow.

From the Mountains to the Sea

A river begins high up at its **source**. The source can be a mountain spring that bubbles up and flows down a mountain's steep sides. The source can also be small streams formed by rainwater that trickle over steep rock. Some rivers begin as mountain marshes or as rainwater seeping through sponge-like rock.

The water at the source of the river is pulled down the mountain slope by the earth's **gravity.** It flows until it reaches a lake or sea. This point is called the river's mouth. The journey between the source and the mouth is the course of a river. More water is added to the river by streams known as **tributaries**.

As the river flows along its course, it carves a channel. The tributaries that feed the river also carve channels. Gravity tries to pull the river down in a straight line, but obstacles help to make the curved shapes of the river landscapes.

Making the channel

Soil and rock is worn away as the river flows, carving out the channel. This process is called **erosion**. Some erosion is caused by the water, but some is caused by bits of rock and soil that are carried along in the flowing water. This rock and soil is called the river's load. The load bumps and scrapes along the channel, wearing it away. This kind of erosion is known as **corrasion**.

Rivers also carry chemicals. Some of these chemicals dissolve soft rock. This type of erosion is called **corrosion**. Corrasion and corrosion often act together to make the course of a river.

A third type of erosion is **attrition**. This is when the rocks and stones on the river bed crash against each other. This breaks the rocks and stones into even smaller pieces.

Changing the channel

Erosion changes the shape and depth of the river's channel all the time. So does **deposition**. This is when the river drops, or deposits, its load of rocks and soil along the way. Deposition mostly occurs when there has been heavy rainfall or a flood of water from ice that has melted higher in the river's course. At these times the river is full and fast-flowing. It carries a lot of eroded material with it. The river drops large rocks and boulders first, high in its course. As the course flattens, the river drops smaller stones. When it reaches the sea, the river deposits fine soil called **silt**.

The mouth of the Mississippi River opens into the Gulf of Mexico. Here the river splits into **bayous.** They are marshy outlets where the water forces itself through the silty deposits. The Mississippi River deposits a tremendous amount of silt every year.

River Landscapes

Rivers **erode** and deposit material all the time. This is because they are finding the easiest, smoothest way toward the sea.

The river profile

The diagram below shows the side view, or profile, of a river as it runs its course. The top line of this side view is very bumpy. This is because the river has worn away soft rock, but cannot wear away the hard rock in its way. The water has to fall over a hard edge as a waterfall. It then has to fill a lake before it trickles over the rocky lip and down toward the sea.

The dotted line shows what the river is trying to do. It is trying to wear away a totally smooth profile. This would give the river an easy journey to its mouth.

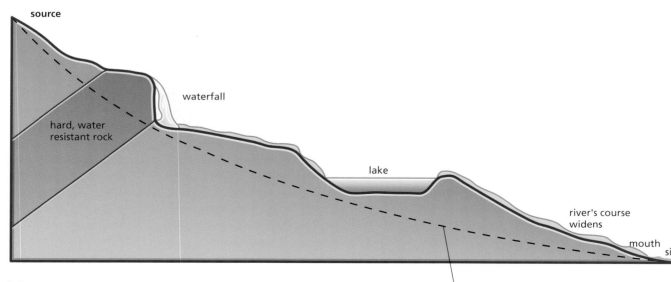

source

waterfall

hard, water resistant rock

lake

river's course widens

mouth

silt

The river is trying to erode a straight flat course, like this.

Shapes in the course

As the river leaves the mountain, it reaches the valley floor, which it has helped to carve. Here it **scours** out its channel in the softest rock. It often flows quickly as rapids over bands and outcrops of hard rock. The river drops some of its load as it flows.

Further along, the valley floor gets flatter and the river gets a bit slower. This part is called the river **flood plain**. Here, even more of the load is dumped. The water struggles to move through the river's deposits as it moves in curves around the deposits and hard rock. These curves are called **meanders**. Rivers make many different shapes in the earth and rock.

When the neck of a meander gets very narrow, the river water begins to flow straight over it. The loop gets cut off, leaving a lake called a cut-off or an oxbow.

Where the river meets the sea

When the river joins the sea, it flows very slowly, and its load of fine **silt** finally sinks. The sluggish water has to make its way around these deposits. As it does so, it splits into streams called **distributaries**. This low-lying plain of distributaries and silt is called a **delta**. Sometimes, islands are formed where distributaries flow around a large bank of silt.

The Mighty Nile

The Nile River is the longest river in the world. It flows along the east side of Africa for 4,160 miles (6,693 kilometers). Its **source** is in the Ruwenzori mountain range in Tanzania. The river flows north from Lake Victoria until it reaches Egypt and the Mediterranean Sea. The Nile has carved huge features in the landscape all along its course. It flows through different types of **climate** and vegetation.

The course of the Nile

The river profile on page 12 shows a simple course. There is just one waterfall and one lake as that river makes its way to the sea.

Many different types of boats sail along the wide, deep parts of the Nile River. These small trading vessels are called feluccas.

The map on this page shows that the Nile has a long, complicated course. There are many **tributary** rivers, waterfalls, and lakes. There are long stretches of turbulent waters that run over huge boulders in the river channel. These stretches are called **cataracts**. The river flows into lakes and then out of them again. It passes through a great swamp known as the Sudd. The Nile has thousands of small **meanders**. It also has two huge bends that pass through the Nubian Desert.

Different climates

The Nile is so long that it flows through different climates. Like most rivers, the Nile has a high, cool source in the mountains. The Nile then passes through warm, wet forests until it reaches the **flood plain**, where the temperatures are very hot and dry. At the coast, there are cool, wet winters and hot, dry summers. This is known as a Mediterranean climate.

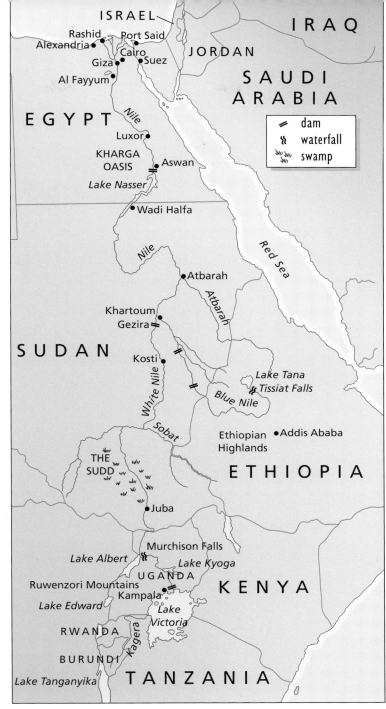

This map shows the locations of man-made dams that have been designed to help people use the river. People have also stopped some of the waterfalls to make the course of the river smoother.

River Plants

Where river plants grow

Flowing water is known as a **lotic habitat** for plants and animals. Many plants have **adapted** well to living in it. But large river plants do not grow easily near cold mountain waterfalls. They cannot grow well in shallow, fast-flowing rivers with stony beds, either. Here, mosses and tiny **algae** grow best because they hug the rocks. Algae are the simplest form of plant life. They have a jelly-like coating that reduces the rubbing action, or friction, of the flowing water. Small mosses cling with grips that are in line with the flowing **current.** This keeps the water from tearing the mosses away from the rocks.

The bulrush is a member of the reed-mace family. It grows in shallow fresh water in many parts of the world. Bulrushes grow between 5 and 8 feet (1.5 and 2.5 meters) tall. They have strong stems with a waxy coating that protects them from the water. Their flowers are tiny and tightly packed into a long plume, and their leaves are wide, waxy, and very tough. Bulrushes absorb a lot of moisture. This moisture **evaporates** through tiny holes in the leaves. Bulrush leaves can be woven into baskets. The fleshy pulp inside the stem is dried and made into rope.

Along the warmer **flood plain**, the river bed often has very fine, deep, rich soil. So do the marshes that spread out from the river. Here, many larger plants have been able to adapt to life in and around the water. Still or slower flowing water is known as a **lentic** habitat.

The water hyacinth comes from South America, but it has spread to North America and Australia. It has blue flowers with yellow spots. These form a spike set high above the water. The leaf-stalks have many air pockets. They help the plant float well above the surface. The stems are strong to cope with the flowing water. They have many fibers. The fibers can be made into paper or dried and used for fuel. The water hyacinth is also known as the million-dollar weed. This is because it has cost millions of dollars to stop it from clogging **river systems** in the southern United States.

River Animals

All sorts of mammals, amphibians, reptiles, birds, fish, and insects live in the world's rivers. Most **species** live in the calmer waters of the **flood plain** and marshlands. But others have adapted to fast-flowing waters higher in the river's course. They have **adapted** their bodies to cope with the impact of the rushing water. Blackfly **larvae**, for example, have hooks and suckers so they can attach themselves firmly to rocks.

Living in the river

Some mammals, such as beavers, have developed webbed feet that help them swim in the water. So have amphibians, such as frogs, and waterbirds, such as ducks. Crocodiles swim by swinging their long powerful tails from side to side.

What is this animal with a duck's bill, webbed feet, a furry body, and a squashed tail? It is a mammal called the duck-billed platypus. It lives in southern Australia and Tasmania. The female digs burrows in the riverbank and lays her eggs in a nest made of weeds, leaves, and grass. The platypus uses its flat tail and webbed feet to swim. Its long bill stirs up the mud at the bottom of the river. This uncovers the platypus's food of insects, worms, and shellfish.

River mammals can hold their breath underwater for a long time, which makes it easier to find food. Amphibians spend part of their lives in water, where they breathe through gills. Fish use their skin and gills on the sides of their heads to breathe. Reptiles can stay in the water for a long time, but they breathe in air above the water.

Most river animals use their large mouths to catch their prey or bite off river plants. The crocodile floats in shallow water, where it snatches its prey. Then the crocodile drags the prey into deep water. A crocodile can close its nostrils very tightly. Its ears have flaps that shut out water. And it can cover its eyes with a third eyelid that allows it to see underwater.

The Atlantic salmon lives in parts of the Atlantic Ocean. When it is time to breed, it swims upriver, using its strong muscles to leap against fast-flowing rapids. The female makes a nest in the stony bed of a mountain stream. She lays as many as 20,000 eggs and covers them with stones and **silt**. The adult fish then return to the sea. The young salmon hatch and stay in the river for about two years. Then they go down to the sea until it is time for them to return to the river to breed.

Living with the River

For thousands of years, rivers have provided drinking water, food, and well-watered farmland. Riverside plants have been used as materials for building homes both in and around the water.

People have made boats from river reeds, wood, and tree bark. The waters provide a way of transporting goods and people to other settlements.

Rivers have protected people against their enemies. Many old towns and villages were built where a **tributary** joins the main river. This was even better for protection and transportation. Some ancient settlements were built inside the loop of a **meander**. This meant that only one wall needed to be built to protect the community. Many rivers also provide a natural border between countries, such as the Rio Grande, which marks the border between the United States and Mexico. Rivers are so important that they have become part of the religion of many people.

Steamboats helped the river port of New Orleans to grow. This city curves around a bend near the mouth of the Mississippi River. Ships sail from here to the Gulf of Mexico along channels that have been **dredged** to make them deeper. The settlement began as a group of Native American villages. More than 200 years ago, New Orleans began to **export** crops, such as cotton, to other parts of the world. It is still a major shipping center.

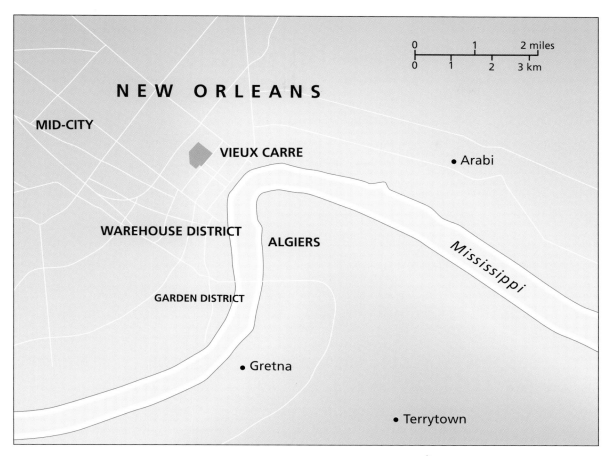

Rivers can also bring problems, such as flooding. They are also breeding grounds for mosquitoes, which can spread diseases such as malaria.

Cities and civilizations

Some of the greatest cities of the world began as small settlements on rivers. Large boats brought goods and people to the cities. This allowed trade to develop. Later, factories were built in cities near the rivers. Factory owners used ships to bring in **raw materials**, such as cotton. These raw materials were then manufactured into goods.

Great civilizations also developed on the banks of rivers. Ancient Egypt grew on the banks of the Nile River more than 5,000 years ago.

The oldest areas of New Orleans, Louisiana, such as the *Vieux Carre,* or French Quarter, were built around a sharp bend in the Mississippi River. The city now covers a much larger area, including Algiers, on the inside of the meander.

A Way of Life—Bangladesh

Most of Bangladesh lies where the Ganges and Brahmaputra Rivers meet the sea. In this **delta** area, the land is very flat and low lying. During the cool, dry months, the rivers fork out into **distributaries** that make their way to the Indian Ocean. But during the summer months, rain pours down and water flows from the melting snows in the Himalaya Mountains.

This means that there is too much water for the river to hold. The river delta floods, and water covers many square miles of land. Sometimes storm surges create huge

This map shows Bangladesh during the dry winter months, when the rivers flow inside their normal banks. The darker areas of the map are very low-lying. It would look different in the summer, when the delta floods. This is due to heavy rainfall—about 203 inches (508 cm) in the northeast and 56 inches (140 cm) in the east central region.

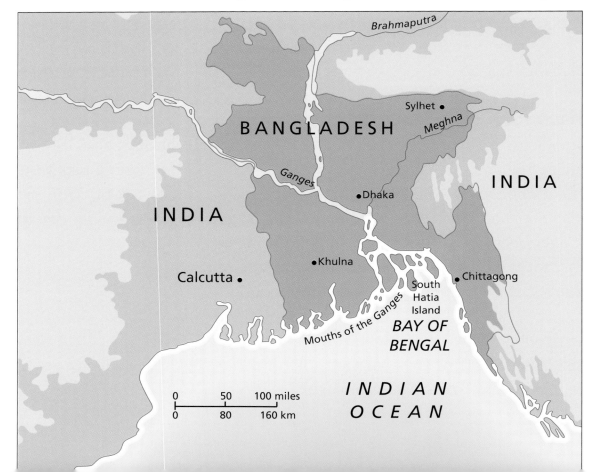

waves that smother the delta in seawater. The flood waters kill many plants. But billions of tiny blue-green **algae** feed on the dead plants and create lots of nitrogen in the soil. This makes the land very **fertile** and good for farming.

Living and working in Bangladesh

The people living on the delta always have to be prepared for flooding. They build their homes on banks or platforms of earth. The houses are usually made of wood and are set on stilts. Even so, flooding often causes many deaths and damage to farmland.

In the dry winters, the ground is full of large holes. This is where the earth was dug up to make the banks and platforms. The holes are called borrow pits. Water fills the pits and is used for drinking and washing. It is also used for **irrigating** crops.

Most people in Bangladesh are farmers. They grow two or three crops of rice each year in the rich, damp soil. They also grow **tropical** fruits, beans, oilseeds, wheat, vegetables, bamboo, and jute. Nearly a million tons of fish are caught every year. Most are freshwater fish.

Bangladesh even gets some of its electricity from rivers. This is called hydroelectric power (HEP).

Jute is grown where the farmland floods. Its stems are woody and have many fibers. The stems can be soaked, dried, and made into rope, sacking, or matting.

Changing Rivers

Rivers change naturally all the time. The way people use rivers changes them, too.

Natural flooding

Flooding happens all the time. It often occurs in spring, when there is a lot of melting snow and ice, or after a very heavy rainfall. After a flood, the river's channel may have changed.

Over the last few years, flooding has increased. There are more floods, and they cause more damage. One of the worst floods in recent years was on the Chang River in China in 1998. Many people lost their lives and homes. But what has made floods so bad? People are partly to blame.

 The waterwheel is an ancient tool for **irrigation.** This one picks up water in the buckets and tips it into the wooden channel that leads to the fields.

Taking the water, changing the flow

Humans have made some of the greatest changes to rivers. One has been the building of dams. Dams are usually built on rivers to store water and to direct it to dry farmland. There are other types of river irrigation. Some use water straight from the river. This changes the way the river **erodes** its channel and deposits material.

Thousands of years ago, river irrigation was used in ancient Egypt, Mesopotamia, China, and Peru. Early Native Americans irrigated more than 380 square miles (1,000 square kilometers) of land in Arizona's Salt River Valley.

The Riaño reservoir in Spain was made to irrigate farmland and to provide power. But the old town of Riaño had to be moved from the **fertile** valley floor to the bare mountainside.

Changing times

Today boats can still sail from the Atlantic Ocean up the Guadalquivir River to the city of Seville, Spain. This is a distance of 50 miles (80 kilometers). But long ago boats were able to reach the city port of Cordoba. This is another 75 miles (100 kilometers) beyond Seville. Over time the river channel filled with **silt**. This silting caused the Donana marshlands, which are now home to many **species** of marshland birds and animals.

Looking to the Future

Dam building, flooding, and pollution are upsetting **river systems** throughout the world. Most of these problems are made by people. We use too much water in our homes and industry and too much energy. We pollute the rain and the rivers. The future of our rivers depends a lot on us.

The problem of dams

Dams have been built for **irrigation** and to help rivers flow all year round. They also provide hydroelectric power (HEP). The cascading water let out through the dam wall turns **turbines** that provide electricity.

But dams can flood villages and river landscapes. They stop the natural flow of rivers. This dries up river systems and destroys the habitat of river wildlife.

Flooding

Floods kill people and destroy homes and farmland. They also alter river channels and systems. Floods have become worse in the last few years. This is partly because storms have become more frequent and more violent.

Many scientists blame this on the world's slightly hotter weather. The increased heat causes more moisture to **evaporate**, which turns into more rain clouds.

Some scientists think the hotter weather is caused by an increase in carbon dioxide and other gases in the atmosphere. These gases trap the sun's heat. They come from sources such as factories and cars. If the earth's temperature rises too much, polar ice could melt and cause even more flooding. All this disrupts the **water cycle** and affects the world's rivers.

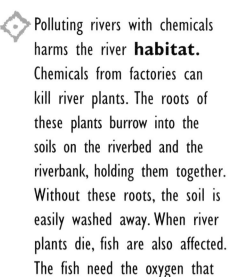

Polluting rivers with chemicals harms the river **habitat.** Chemicals from factories can kill river plants. The roots of these plants burrow into the soils on the riverbed and the riverbank, holding them together. Without these roots, the soil is easily washed away. When river plants die, fish are also affected. The fish need the oxygen that the plants produce.

River Facts

The world's longest rivers

These are the twelve longest rivers in the world. The table shows how long the rivers are, but it does not show how much water drains into each river or how much water flows out through the mouth of the river. This is very difficult to calculate. Scientists estimate that about 1,600 million tons of water are discharged from the Mississippi into the Gulf of Mexico every day.

	Continent	Length (miles)	(kilometers)
Nile	Africa	4,160	6,693
Amazon	South America	4,000	6,436
Chang Jiang (Yangtze)	Asia	3,964	6,378
Mississippi-Missouri	North America	3,710	5,969
Yenisey-Angara	Asia	3,445	5,550
Huang He (Yellow)	Asia	3,395	5,464
Ob-Irtysh	Asia	3,362	5,410
Parana-Plata	South America	2,795	4,500
Amur	Asia	2,744	4,415
Lena	Asia	2,734	4,400
Congo	Africa	2,718	4,373
Mekong	Asia	2,600	4,183

. . . and the shortest

Shortest river with a name—Roe River in Montana. It is only 200 feet (61 meters) long.

Did you know that the Mississippi Delta expands each year by 328 feet (100 meters)?

Polluted rivers

The Cuyahoga River in Ohio became so polluted that in 1952, and again in 1969, it actually caught fire! Since then efforts have been made to clean up polluted rivers.

The Ganges River is a holy river for followers of the Hindu religion. People bathe in the waters at sunrise as part of their daily prayer. When a person dies, his or her ashes are sprinkled on the river.

Glossary

adapt to change to make suitable for a new use

algae simple form of plant life, ranging from a single cell to huge seaweed

atmosphere layer of gases that surrounds the earth

attrition erosion caused by friction or gradual wearing away

bayou marshy stream that forces itself through silt at the river's mouth

cataract waterfall or series of waterfalls

climate rainfall, temperature, and winds that normally affect a large area

corrasion when stones get carried along by flowing water and bump against a river's bed and sides, eroding them away

corrosion when something is gradually eaten away, for example being dissolved by chemicals

current strong surge of water that flows constantly in one direction

delta where a river meets the ocean and the water splits into smaller slow-moving streams

deposition when a river drops its load of rock and silt on the river bed

distributary one of the streams a river separates into when it reaches its delta

drainage basin bowl-shaped area surrounded by higher ground, in which a river and its tributaries flow

dredge to dig out layers of silt from a river bed

erosion wearing away of rocks and soil by wind, water, ice, or acid

evaporate to turn from liquid into vapor, such as when water becomes water vapor

export to sell goods to another country

fertile describes rich soil in which crops can grow easily

fertilizer substance added to soil to make plants grow better

flood plain flat land in a valley that is regularly flooded

gravity force of attraction that exists between any two objects in the universe

habitat place where a plant or animal grows or lives in nature

irrigate to supply a place or area with water to grow crops

larva (more than one are larvae) undeveloped, but active, young of animals such as insects and frogs

lentic slow-moving water habitat for animals and plants

lotic habitat of running water for plants and animals

meander loop in a river's course

plate area of the earth's crust separated from other plates by deep cracks. Earthquakes, volcanic activity, and the forming of mountains take place where these plates meet.

raw materials natural materials that can be made into other things

river system a river and all the tributaries that run into it

scour to rub hard against something, wearing it away

silt fine particles of eroded rock and soil that settle in rivers, sometimes blocking the movement of water

source where a river begins

species one of the groups used for classifying animals. The members of each species are very similar.

trade winds winds that blow steadily towards the equator, but get pulled westward by the rotation of the earth

tributary stream or river that runs into a main river

tropical in or from the Tropics, which is the region between the Tropic of Cancer and the Tropic of Capricorn. These are two imaginary lines drawn around the earth, above and below the equator.

turbine revolving motor that is driven by water or steam and can produce electricity

water cycle system by which the earth's water is constantly changing from rivers, lakes, and seas to water vapor in the air that falls as rain and drains into rivers, lakes, and seas again

watershed area of high ground surrounding a river's drainage basin

water vapor water that has been heated until it forms a gas that is held in the air. Drops of water form again when the vapor is cooled.

More Books to Read

Pirotta, Saviour. *Rivers in the Rain Forest.* Austin, Tex.: Raintree Steck-Vaughn, 1999.

Stephen, Richard. *Rivers.* Mahwah, N.J.: Troll Communications, 1997.

Tesar, Jenny E. *America's Top 10 Rivers.* Woodbridge, Conn.: Blackbirch Press, Inc., 1997.

Index